The Origin of the Giants: The First Settlers of Albion

Bilingual edition

J.S. Mackley

Copyright © 2014 J S Mackley

New Edition 2025

Published by Isengrin Publishing, Northampton

Set in Garamond

All rights reserved. No part of this publication may be reproduced, stored in any retrieval system, or transmitted, in any form or by any means, electronic, mechanical, photocopying, recording or otherwise except for the purpose of academic study, without the prior permission of the publishers.

ISBN: 978-1-917130-08-0

For Katherine Blake and the ladies who give so much to medieval music and literature.

ACKNOWLEDGMENTS

The transcription of this volume is based on the text published by Georgine E. Brereton (1906–1969) published as *Dez Grantz Geanz, Medium Ævum Monographs*, II (Oxford: Blackwell, 1937).

I am grateful to J.W. Mackley for his work on the translation.

DISCUSSION

Introduction

Georgine E. Brereton published the text of Albina and her sisters under the title *Dez Grantz Geanz* in 1937.[1] Written in octo-syllabic rhyming couplets, a popular medium for Anglo-Norman poetry, the story tells of Albina's plot to lead her sisters to murder their husbands. When this plan is discovered, the sisters are exiled, ultimately making landfall on an unnamed, uninhabited land, which Albina names after herself. The devils on the island assume human form and seduce the sisters who give birth to the giants who are the ancestors of those who are discovered when Brutus, great-grandson of Æneas of Troy, settles on the island.

The text of this version is based on MS Cotton Cleopatra D.ix ff. 67ra–68vc which dates from 1332–4 held in the British Library in London.[2] It is the only

---

[1] Georgine E. Brereton, *Dez Grantz Geanz: An Anglo-Norman Poem*, Medium Ævum Monographs II (Oxford: Basil Blackwell, 1937).
[2] Brereton's edition also contains an abridged version taken from Oxford, Bodleian Library MS Rawlinson D. 329.

manuscript that preserves this text as an independent unit, although Brereton lists a further fifteen manuscripts where the text has been abridged or serves as a prologue to a vernacular chronicle of Britain in both prose and verse entitled the *Roman de Brut*, based on Geoffrey's *Historia Regum Britanniae* (*History of the Kings of Britain*). Principal versions of the *Brut* were written in Anglo-Norman by Robert Wace (b. *c*. 1110, d. *c*. 1174) and in Middle English by Laȝamon (writing *c*. 1190). An abridged version of *Deȝ Grantȝ Geanȝ* was translated into Latin as *De origine gigantum*.

Other editions

There are two earlier editions, noted by Brereton, although she observes that 'neither reproduced [the text] with accuracy'.[3]

- o Achille Jubinal 'Des graunz jaianz qui primes conquistrent Bretaigne' in *Nouveau recueil des contes, dits, fabliaux, et autres pièces inédites* (Paris: Chez Challamel, 1842), vol. 2, pp. 354-71 (omitting lines 378, 379).

- o François Michel, 'De Primis Inhabitatoribus Angliæ' in *Gesta Regum Britanniae*, (London: Cambrian Archaeological Association, 1862), pp. 199–214.

---

[3] Brereton, *Deȝ Grantȝ Geanȝ*, p. v.

More recently, James P. Carley and Julia Crick published an edition of the abridged Anglo-Norman version with a parallel text from the Latin version, *De origine gigantum* which was updated by Ruth Evans:

o James P. Carley and Julia Crick, 'Constructing Albion's Past: an Annotated Edition of *De Origine Gigantum*', in *Arthurian Literature* XIII (1995): 41–114, pp. 92–113.

o Ruth Evans, Gigantic Origins: An Annotated translation of *De Origine Gigantum*', *Arthurian Literature* XVI (1998): 197–211.

The manuscript

Contents of London, British Library, Cotton Cleopatra, D.ix

Ms Cotton Cleopatra D.ix is a miscellany of booklets and folios. Brereton observes that 'the MS is composed of three originally separate articles of which the first (ff. 2–86) alone concerns us here'.[4] Johnson notes that the first article is comprised of five separate booklets.[5] The majority of these are in Latin although there are texts in Anglo-Norman and Middle English. *Deȝ Grantȝ Geanȝ* is found at ff.67r–68v; it is the only part of the manuscript made up of three, rather than two, columns.

---

[4] Brereton, *Deȝ Grantȝ Geanȝ*, p. vi.
[5] Lesley Johnson, 'Return to Albion', in *Arthurian Literature* XIII (1995): 19–40, p. 39.

f.2r–21v *Annales ab initio mundi ad annum 1292* (annals from the beginning of the world to 1292)

f.22r–34v *Libellus de summis pontificibus Romanae ecclesiae, a S. Petro ad Johannem XXII AD 1317* (A booklet listing the Popes from St Peter to John XXII, (d. 1317))

f.35r–65v *Annales de gestis Anglorum a morte Hegnisti ad Ann. 1377* (Annals of the feats of the English from the death of Hengist to 1377)

f.67r-68v *Rythmi in veteri lingua Gallicana,[6] de primis incolis Britanniae* (rhymed verse in old French dialect, of the first inhabitants of Britain)

f.69r–71r *Compendium de archiepiscopis Cantuariensibus a S. Augustino ad Johannem de Stratford* (A list of the Archbishops of Canterbury, from Augustine to the investiture of John of Stratford (1333))

f.71v-75r *Thomae Chesterfeld canonici Lichfeldiensis historia de episcopis Coventriensibus et Lichfeldiensibus, a prima fundatione ecclesiae ad Ann. 1347* (Thomas Chesterfield, Canon of Lichfield, history of the bishopric of Coventry and Lichfield from the earliest foundation of the church to the year 1347. (Additional material in a later hand to 1388).

---

[6] Roger Bacon, writing in 1260, identified four separate 'gallicana' dialects, namely, Norman, Burgundian Picardian and Parisian (*Compendium Studii philosophiae*, VI, 478, cited in R. Anthony Lodge, *French: From Dialect to Standard* (London: Routledge, 1993) p. 97.

THE ORIGIN OF THE GIANTS

Other materials in the manuscript are collected in separate gatherings including a brief chronicle arranged by year from King William I to the year 1314, fragments of orders and letters regarding the civil wars during the reign of Edward II, the *Speculum* of Edward III from Simon Islip Archbishop of Canterbury, and sections from the *South English Legendary* and *Miracles of the Virgin*.

The date of MS Cotton Cleopatra D. ix is attested by the textual evidence: the second folio bears the inscription *Liber Alani de Assheburne Vicarii Lichf*, which refers to Alan of Ashbourne, vicar of Lichfield Cathedral who died in 1334.[7] The manuscript also contains a list of archbishops of Canterbury from Augustine to the death of Simon de Meopham and the investiture of John of Stratford in 1333. Consequently, Brereton argues that 'the date of this MS. can be fixed with certainty' to 1333-4. This date is challenged by Lesley Johnson, James P. Carley and Julia Crick who observe that the *obit* of Simon of Meopham 'is a later addition' which may have been added to the notice of his consecration in 1328. Carley and Crick further observe that the last date in the chronicle that ends on fol. 67v is 1332, while the chronicle that follows this story begins on 1333.[8]

---

[7] Brereton, *Dez Grantz Geanz*, p. vi. MS. Oxford, Bodleian Library Ashmole 794 has an entry for the year 1335 describing a mass said *anno ultimo pro anima Alani de Assheburne*.

[8] James P. Carley and Julia Crick, 'Constructing Albion's Past: an Annotated Edition of *De Origine Gigantum*', in *Arthurian Literature*

Lisa Ruch argues that the emphasis on nobility in the first third of *Des Grantz Geanz* suggests that it was originally aimed at an aristocratic audience.[9] Brereton argues that the dialect is 'typically Anglo-Norman and together with the occasional use of English words and the incorrectness of the versification they form an unmistakable indication of insular origin', that is, composed in England, rather than on the continent. That said, *Des Grantz Geanz* contains some language that is 'characteristic of the continental influence of the thirteenth century'. Brereton compares it to a middle thirteenth century text *Boeve de Haumtone* (*Bevis of Hampton*) and argues that the composition of *Des Grantz Geanz* was "not earlier than the beginning – probably not before the middle – of the thirteenth century", and the textual evidence of MS A shows that it was written around 1328–34.[10] Thus the text was likely to have been written between *c*.1250 and 1334.

XIII (1995): 41–114, p. 46; Lesley Johnson, 'Return to Albion', in *Arthurian Literature* XIII (1995): 19–40, p. 23.

[9] Lisa M. Ruch, *Albina and her Sisters: The Foundation of Albion* (New York: Cambria Press, 2013), p. 65.

[10] Brereton, *Dez Grantz Geanz*, p. xxxii

THE ORIGIN OF THE GIANTS

Geoffrey of Monmouth and the Historia Regum Brittaniae

Dez Grantz Geanz is a response to one of the first episodes of Geoffrey of Monmouth's *Historia Regum Britanniae* which was written in Latin around 1135–38.[11] This latter text covers almost two thousand years, chronicling the line of ninety-nine kings from the first settlers on the island to the death of the last British King, Cadwallader.

From the little surviving written evidence from before Geoffrey, we can piece together a series of documents that influenced the Albina legend. The earliest surviving description of the Britons is in the form of a sermon written by Gildas the Wise (*c.* 500–*c.* 570) entitled *De Excidio et Conquesto Britanniae* (*On the Ruin and Conquest of Britain*). He presents a factual account of some contemporary events; however, the text is not intended as a history, but as a condemnation of the acts of five kings. While having no direct bearing on the Albina legend, Gildas's description of the island of Britain directly influenced Bede's *Historia ecclesiastica gentis Anglorum* (*The Ecclesiastical History of the English People*) which was composed around 731 and which, in spite of the title, was written as a description of the development of the Church in Britain rather than the people. More

---

[11] For biographical details for Geoffrey see Karen Jankulak, *Geoffrey of Monmouth* (Cardiff: University of Wales Press, 2010), also Michael Reeve, 'Introduction' in Geoffrey of Monmouth, *The History of the Kings of Britain*, ed. Michael D. Reeve, trans. Neil Wright (Woodbridge: The Boydell Press, 2007), p. vii.

importantly, Gildas influenced Nennius's *Historia Brittonum* (*History of the Britons*) which includes details of the Trojans fleeing Troy and Brutus's arrival in Britain. In this version of the legend, Nennius names the character as 'Britto', although he does also refer to 'Brutus the Hateful'.

On three occasions, Geoffrey claims that he is translating from a 'very old book in the British tongue' that was given to him by Walter, Archdeacon of Oxford.[12] Such a book has never been discovered. However, Guy Halsall observes that Geoffrey never once quotes directly from the 'old book' whereas he falsely attributes some of his source material to Gildas and Bede, some of which he also 'adapts, modifies and contradicts … at will' and on other occasions, he lifts lengthy passages without attribution to his source.[13] Geoffrey is more reliant on Gildas than Bede, but he particularly draws on scenes from Nennius.

---

[12] 'Britannici sermonis librum uetustissimum', Geoffrey, *History*, p. 4.
[13] Guy Halsall, *Worlds of Arthur* (Oxford: Oxford University Press, 2013), p. 142; Martin Aurell, 'Geoffrey of Monmouth's History of the Kings of Britain and the Twelfth-Century Renaissance' in Stephen Morillo (ed.) *The Haskins Society Journal*, vol. 18 (Woodbridge, The Boydell Press, 2006): 1–18, p. 7.

The Origin of the Giants

The Founding of Britain in the Historia Regum Brittaniae

After the siege of Troy, Æneas fled Troy with his son Ascanius. They settled in Italy and finds favour with King Latinus of Italy (King of the Latins). Turnus, King of the Rutuli, is envious of the attention shown to Æneas by Lavinia, daughter of Latinus. Turnus attacks, but is defeated by Æneas, who is then granted overlordship of Italy and he marries Lavinia.[14] After Æneas's death, he is succeeded by Ascanius, who has a son named Silvius.

Silvius marries a niece of Lavinia, and when she becomes pregnant, Ascanius orders a magician to deduce the sex of the baby, whereupon it is prophesied that the child would kill his mother and his father. This prophecy is proved true as his mother dies in childbirth and the young Brutus accidentally kills his father when out hunting; Brutus is thus exiled from Italy. He travels to Greece where he frees many descendants of survivors from Troy. Together they travel to an island called Leogeia where they discover a temple to Diana where Æneas receives a prophecy that he will travel to a deserted island 'where giants once lived' and where he would establish a new Troy and 'From your descendants will arise kings, who will be masters of the whole world'.[15]

Based on this prophecy, the Trojans travel around the

---

[14] Geoffrey *History*, p. 6. Cf, Virgil, *The Aeneid*, Bks VII, IX, X, XII.
[15] Geoffrey *History*, p. 20.

Mediterranean where they discover more Trojan exiles, led by Corineus. Next, they travel to Aquitaine and the Loire, finally coming ashore at Totnes on the island of Albion. However, Diana's prophecy proves incorrect: the island is still inhabited by 'a few giants'. The Trojans begin to cultivate the land, driving the giants away to mountain caves. Brutus then names the island after himself, and gives overlordship of the southernmost country to Corineus, who also names it Cornwall after himself.

A 'monster' called Goemagog leads twenty giants to attack the Britons who are celebrating their feast for the gods, inflicting terrible carnage. The Britons counter-attack killing all the giants save Goemagog whom Brutus spares 'because he wanted to see him wrestle with Corineus'.

After a graphic fight, Corineus hauls Goemagog onto his shoulders and carries him to a 'nearby shore' where the giant is hurled out to sea and falls 'down the rocky crag [where] the giant was torn into a thousand pieces and stained the sea red with his blood'.[16] This place was then called 'Goemagog's Leap': it is traditionally believed to be Plymouth Hoe, and indeed chalk figures of 'two men with clubbes' were carved into the turf until the building of the citadel on Plymouth Hoe in 1671.[17]

---

[16] Geoffrey, *History*, p. 28. The full text of Brutus's arrival in Albion and the defeat of the giants has been included as an appendix.

[17] Thomas Westcote, *View of Devonshire in MDCXXX with a Pedigree of Most of its Gentry* (Exeter: William Roberts, 1845), p. 383.

The Origin of the Giants

Thus, according to Geoffrey, Brutus and Corineus rid the land of the indigenous population. Brutus then travels the land and establishes his capital on the banks of the river Thames which he calls New Troy, but which eventually becomes London.

This legend of Brutus and the Trojans as the first settlers of Britain was well-known in the centuries after Geoffrey was writing and was accepted as history. Geoffrey takes the story of Æneas and his descendants almost verbatim from Nennius's *Historia Britonnum* written around 830; Geoffrey also adds a later section of the *Historia* to provide further detail to Brutus's travels and to give him a status to equal Æneas. Nennius's was drawing on a common literary trope that was well-known in Classical literature. It is mentioned by, amongst others, Virgil, Livy and Ammianus Marcellinus. However, Nennius does not include any details of what happens once the Trojans arrive in Albion; specifically, he does not mention the giants. The legend of the giants is not found in any other (surviving) source and is likely to have been Geoffrey's invention. The names of Gog and Magog are found in the Bible – most particularly in Revelation 20:8: they are the followers of Antichrist and symbolic of all future enemies of the Kingdom of God. Fusing the two names together enhanced the magnitude of Corineus's opponent.[18]

---

[18] The different texts use a different form of the name: Geoffrey uses Goemagog; Wace's *Brut* uses Goemagot and *Dez Grantz Geanz* uses Gogmagog.

Geoffrey's tale left questions for later writers to consider: why had Britain originally been called Albion? Where had the giants come from, especially when Diana's prophecy had foretold that the land had been empty? At least one hundred and fifty years after Geoffrey wrote his *Historia*, these details were provided by *Dez Grantz Geanz* which was a stand-alone text. The abridged version became a prologue for the first Anglo-Norman prose *Brut* chronicle, dating from the beginning of the fourteenth century, and thus the gaps in the narrative were explained.[19]

The Albina story

The principal story of *Dez Grantz Geanz* can be broken into five major parts: (i) The sisters' plot (ll. 1–156); (ii) the judgment and the punishment of being set adrift (ll. 157–234); (iii) the arrival on the island (235–398); (iv) the demons (399–484); and (v) the link with Geoffrey of Monmouth (485–562).

(i) The Sisters' plot (ll. 1–156)

After an appeal to authority, and placing the story into historical context (3970 years after God created the world),[20] the narrator recounts how the King of Greece

---

[19] Julia Marvin, 'Albine and Isabelle: Regicidal Queens and the Historical Imagination of the Anglo-Norman Prose *Brut* Chronicles' in *Arthurian Literature* XVIII (2001): 143–91, p 144.

[20] The age of the world was calculated by adding the ages of the Old Testament Patriarchs together – the *Anglo-Saxon Chronicle* entry for

THE ORIGIN OF THE GIANTS

is master over all other kings on account of his nobility and virtue. He has thirty daughters, although the only one to be named is 'Albine'. This name is included in *Dez Grantz Geanz* to explain Geoffrey and Wace's use of the name 'Albion'.[21] The sisters consider their father's authority as their right as well, and consequently, when their father marries them all to noble kings, they consider that they too should have mastery over their lord rather than submitting to their husbands. Thus they plan their husbands' murder 'In private in their arms, when he would most expect to have comfort' (*Privément entre ses braz, Quant meux quide aver solaz* ll. 71–2).

Consequently, the sisters are noted for their 'pride' and 'arrogance' and 'wicked deeds (*orgoil, fierté* and *grant outrage* ll. 36, 37, 40) which establishes them as the tragic protagonists who must fall. The youngest daughter, overcome by guilt, reveals the sisters' plan to her husband who swiftly informs the sisters' father.

The nationality of the king and number of sisters varies depending on the version of the story. Sometimes the sisters succeed in their plan. There is another version where the Syrian king, Diodicias, had thirty-three daughters who were successful in their plan of cutting their husbands' throats. The source for the story of the murderous sisters parallels the legend of the Danaids, which is found in Apollodorus's *Bibliotheca* (II.I.15), Ovid's

---

AD 6 announces the that the earth was 5200 years old.
[21] Brereton, *Dez Grantz Geanz*, p. xxxiv.

Heroides (xiv) and Horace's *Odes* (III.xi). In the classical version, the fifty daughters of Danaus, King of Argos, were to marry the fifty sons of Aegyptus, Danaus's twin brother. The sisters plot to murder their husbands on their wedding night at their father's command. All carry out the murder except for Hypermnestra whose husband respected her wish to remain a virgin.[22]

(ii) The punishment of being set adrift (158–234)

The violent murder planned by the sisters is met by the cold, judiciary nature of the court. The king, their father, sides with the husbands and the punishment is based on their noble lineage. However, while the judges decree that the sisters should suffer exile rather than execution, the nature of the punishment – being set adrift without means of steering the vessel and without food – their chances of survival were seriously reduced and consequently, it falls to providence as to whether the condemned survive or not.[23] Reinhard observes that 'setting adrift was a penalty assigned in those cases wherein the evidence of guilt was not or could not be conclusive in the eyes of a human judge ... or in which it

---

[22] Cf. Tamar Drukker, 'Thirty-Three Murderous Sisters: A Pre-Trojan Foundation Myth in the Middle English Brut Chronicle', *The Review of English Studies*, New Series, Vol. 54 (2003): 449–63.

[23] Cf. Mary E Byrne, 'On the Punishment of Sending Adrift', *Èriu* 11 (1932): 97–102.

was desirable to temper justice with mercy'.[24] At this stage, the sisters had not actually committed a crime, they had simply planned it. According to Reinhard, intent 'was itself held to be criminal and hence liable to a penalty.'[25]

The ship is 'big and strong', clearly seaworthy despite the absence of a rudder, thus the sisters will be carried to wherever fate takes them. In addition there is no food on board. Consequently, although this is not an *actual* death sentence, the judges have effectively condemned the sisters to an excruciatingly painful end through starvation and dehydration. In addition, it is noted 'No one had any pity on them' (l. 192) and while the narrative describes the effect of hunger, this is forgotten by the tempests that threaten the boat. The violence of the storm mirrors the planned murder of the husbands as well as anticipating the violence of the giants. However, if Albina was set adrift in Greece, then her vessel must have followed a similar route to that of Brutus.

If Albina and her sisters represent the Danaids, then the punishment of being set adrift without means of steering the boat may well reflect the punishment inflicted on Danaë, mother of Perseus, who was cast away in a chest, and who was a descendant of Hypermnestra. Survival meant that the gods were protecting them. Cohen suggests that 'this particular

---

[24] J.R. Reinhard, 'Setting adrift in Medieval Law and Literature', *PMLA* 56 (1941): 33–68, p. 47.

[25] Reinhard, 'Setting adrift', p. 53.

punishment is traditionally reserved for incestuous daughters and women who have given birth to monsters, anticipating the sisters' ultimate fate'.[26]

iii) the arrival on the island (235–398)

The storm that carries the sisters to the unnamed island abates, leaving their vessel on the shore. By contrast to the dramatic descriptions of the boat being tossed on the waves, the account of the land is much more serene, and from the beginning the language becomes that of a legal register: being the eldest sister and the first to make landfall, Albina claims her control of the land (*Tut premereine en saillant, La terre prist tut en estant*, ll. 254–5). Albina's register is that of feudal terminology when she discusses her authority with her sisters, including *seysin'*, meaning 'possession' (l. 334); *feffee* (l. 346), another feudal term referring to someone who holds an estate in the land, and also *avowé* (ll. 330, 340) is particularly legalistic as it is the feminine form of a feudal lord. And just as the daughters did not object to Albina's plan for them to murder their husbands, so they do not challenge her authority in naming the land.

The land is explored only after it has been named, which contrasts with Brutus who names the land only once it has been explored. That said, the descriptions of this new land in *Dez Granz Geanz* – wild beasts in the

---

[26] Cohen, *On Giants*, p. 48.

forests, streams full of fish – are likely to have been influenced by the descriptions of Britain found in Geoffrey's *Historia* (chapters 5 and 21 in particular). The land is abundant with produce, although Albina notes that they want for nothing, aside from meat (*mes qe viande n'i faut riens*, l. 354) and they quickly tire of eating fruit. The narrator observes that previously they would have had bows, falcons, and dogs to assist with the hunting, but now they must rely on their own ingenuity by making snares and traps. The narrator points out how the sisters 'deceive' the animals (*Dunt les bestes decevoient* l. 383). This alludes to the plots against their husbands where the sisters planned to attack when their husbands least expected it. In effect, the sisters become parodies of the goddess Diana, whose prophecy directs the Trojans to Britain's shores. However, as Anke Bernau observes, Albina's founding of the land differs from that of Brutus in that the sisters 'are closely associated with the landscape': they live in caves and eat fruit and animals. In addition to (re-)naming the land, Brutus builds the city of New Troy.[27]

(iv) the demons (399–484)

The gluttony of the previous scene links directly with the lechery that follows: the women 'became big and fat. Natural lust arouses them disproportionately' (*Grosses e*

---

[27] Anke Bernau, 'Beginning with Albina: Remembering the Nation', *Exemplaria* 21 (2009): 247–73.

grasses deveneient. La chaline de nature Les soumount a desmesure ll. 400–02). From their consequent union with the native spirits, the giants are born. They, in turn, commit incest with their mothers and then between sisters and brothers.

The episode of the giants is clearly drawn from the details of the giants found in Geoffrey's *Historia*. However, their inclusion in *Deȝ Grantȝ Geanȝ* draws on Biblical tradition that was very popular in the literature of the Middle Ages. In the Douay Rheims Bible, written in Latin, Genesis 6:4 describes how before the Great Flood 'giants were upon the earth in those days' (*Gigantes autem erant super terram in diebus illis*). The Hebrew word for giant is *Nephilim*, thus some translations of Genesis 6:4 read

> The Nephilim were on the earth in those days—and also afterward—when the sons of God went to the daughters of humans and had children by them.
> They were the heroes of old, men of renown.

This ambiguous phrase refers to an earlier legend from the First book of Enoch which describes how 'watcher' angels (called *Grigori*) desired and impregnated the daughters of men who gave birth to giants (called *Nephilim*) that are three hundred cubits tall. They initially eat all the humans' food, and when that runs out, they eat the humans as well.[28]

The description of the angels who 'desired' the human women clearly parallels the events in *Deȝ Grantȝ Geanȝ*. Julia Marvin sees the incestuous relationship between mother and son as rape and 'the final humiliation' of the

---

[28] The passage from 1 Enoch 6 and 7 is included as Appendix 2.

sisters, rather than as a further example of their degrading themselves.

The presence of the giants in Geoffrey's *Historia* is potentially as an abomination against God – particularly with the amalgamation of Apocalyptic names. In the same way that the narrator uses the term *avowée* as a feudal term to describe Albina's 'lordship' over her sisters, the same term is used for Gogmagog to discuss his mastery over the other indigenous giants. While the sisters may have been saved from an ignoble death because of their lineage, the giants are condemned to a life of violence and savagery because of *their* heritage. Effectively, the giants represent all that is ignoble about the sisters, a trait which needed to be eradicated by the conquering Trojans over the following 260 years.

v) link with Geoffrey of Monmouth

The presence of the giants is obviously derived from Geoffrey's *Historia*. The question of where they initially came from is the focus of *Dez Grantz Geanz*. However, the presence of the sisters is totally overshadowed by the presence of the giants, although in the First Book of Enoch, the populations are consumed when food runs out – we may consider that this might have been the fate of Albina and her sisters. In Geoffrey's version, the giants are initially driven away by the Trojans, they are not killed. When they return, they both interrupt the holy festivals and 'inflict terrible carnage' on the Britons, forcing the settlers to retaliate. Corineus's wrestling with Goemagog is no more than a show of Briton strength (although it is no easy contest as Goemagog breaks three of Corineus's ribs during the battle). Geoffrey describes how Goemagog is thrown from a place called 'Goemagog's Leap' (*Saltus Goemagog*), although this location is in Plymouth, some 24 miles from Totnes, suggesting that Geoffrey was not completely familiar with Devonian geography. That said, there is no direct reference to the wrestling match taking place in Totnes; in addition, as Theo Brown observes, 'the shores of Totnes' may refer to 'the whole area of South Devon, between Berry Head and Prawle Point'.[29]

The principal difference between Geoffrey's *Historia* and *De Grantz Geanz* is that Geoffrey depicts the giants as uncivilised brutes that disrupt the Trojans' holy ceremonies. They are cunning and able to regroup to attack the Britons (and indeed later in the text, Geoffrey refers to Stonehenge as 'the dance of giants' (*chorea gigantum*).[30] Brutus spares Goemagog for the purpose of seeing the wrestling match (or just the show of strength) between Corineus and Goemagog. The giants are never given a voice. By contrast, in *Dez Grantz Geanz*, Brutus spares Gogmagog to give him the opportunity to tell his

---

[29] Theo Brown, 'The Trojans in Devon', *Report and Transactions of the Devonshire Association for the Advancement of Science, Literature and Art* (1955): 63–76, p. 66.

[30] Geoffrey, *History*, pp. 172–3.

tale.³¹ The root of the word *monster* is from the Latin *monere* – "to warn". Consequently, Gogmagog's narrative may serve as a didactic message against the sins of pride, gluttony and lechery.

Johnson observes that 'Gogmagog's ability to produce a coherent narrative of his own origins works against the projection of the giant community as one of non-civilised aliens.'³² The story could then be saved for future audiences, as the narrator at the beginning of the poem explains 'I heard it from a wise man who was very familiar with the writings about the happenings in olden times' (ll. 10–12). Johnson notes that 'Brutus's act of foundation could be seen as providing a corrective to the earlier, transgressive act of female foundation (brought about, in part, by the refusal of the Greek princesses to cede to the authority of their husbands) which had resulted in a savage and monstrous community'.³³ The coming of the Trojans represents a civilised colonisation of a barbaric land where the inhabitants are the offspring of demons. At the same time, we see the Britons, descendants of the Trojans, defeat giants, descendants of the Greeks and establishing themselves as the dominant authority in the western world.

---

³¹ Corineus does not feature in *Deȝ Grantȝ Geanȝ*.
³² Johnson, 'Return to Albion', pp. 30-1.
³³ Johnson, 'Return to Albion', p. 26.

Dez Grantz Geanz and Wace's *Roman de Brut*

Wace's *Roman de Brut draws* on Geoffrey's *Historia* as well as the works of William of Malmesbury, Henry of Huntingdon and Geoffrey Gaimar. Wace translated certain episodes from Geoffrey of Monmouth, although Judith Weiss observes that while Wace adhered to Geoffrey's outline, he 'felt free to amplify and embellish' the details.[34] The author of *Dez Grantz Geanz* uses phrases directly from the *Roman de Brut* on three occasions. For example, the opening passage of the *Brut*:

> Ki vult oïr e vult saveir
> De rei en rei e d'eir en eir
> Ki cil furent e dunt il vindrent
> Ki Engleterre primes tinderent (*Brut* ll. 1–4)

And those of *Dez Grantz Geanz*:

> Ci put hom saver coment
> E quant e de quele gent
> Les grantz geantz primes vindrent
> Qi Engletere primes tindrent, (*DGG* ll. 1–4)

Later, when discussing the Trojans arriving at Totnes, the *Brut* describes

> Des nés a terre fors eissirent
> Mult furent lied, grant joie firent
> De la terre qu'il unt trovee (*Brut* ll. 1057–9)

---

[34] Judith Weiss (ed. and trans), *Wace's Roman de Brut: A History of the British*, Revised ed. (Exeter: University of Exeter Press, 2002), p. xviii.

The Origin of the Giants

While the corresponding passage of the sisters making landfall describes

> Grant joie trestotes eurent
> Qe si pres de tere furent.
> Tantost de la nef issirent, (*DGG* ll. 247–9)

But in both texts, they find the land deserted, and the description is almost identical:

> Home ne feme n'i troverent (*Brut* l. 622)

> Home ne femme ne troverent (*DGG* l. 622

Finally, in *Dez Grantz Geanz*, when Albina arrives on the land, she gives it her own name

> Deit la terre estre nomee.
> Albine est mon propre noun,
> Dunt serra nomé Albion ; (*DGG* ll.345–9)

This naming process is drawn from Wace's Brut, who acknowledges the original name Albion when it comes to be changed by Brutus:

> La terre aveit nun Albion
> Mais Brutus li chanja sun nun
> De Bruto, sun nun, nun li mist
> E Bretainne apeler la fist (*Brut* ll. 1175–80)

(The country was called Albion, but Brutus changed its name, calling it after his own, and he had called it Britain).

Thus we see there are areas where Wace's *Roman de Brut* directly influenced the text of *Dez Grantz Geanz*, effectively giving authority to the developing legend. The text also relied on other popular legends to explain the origins of the giants.

The wider legends of the Nephilim and the Grigori

According to the Book of Enoch, the Watcher Angels (*Grigori*) taught mankind the forbidden knowledge of (amongst others) sword making, astrology and astronomy. These, along with sexual perversions between the giants (*Nephilim*), led to the attempt to wipe out this knowledge and activity through the Great Deluge. Jeffrey Jerome Cohen suggests that the Nephilim represent 'the transgression of divine laws governing the exogamy in the Hebrew Bible'.[35] That said, there are still Biblical stories of giants in the postdiluvian world, including Goliath and Og of Bashan. Likewise, when writing in the ninth century, Wulfstan II, Archbishop of York, claims in a homily entitled 'De falsis deis' that 'Nembroð and ða etnas worhton þone wundorlican stypel æfter Noes flode' (Nimrod and the giants built the wonderful tower [of Babel] after Noah's flood, ll. 5-6).[36] All of this suggests that the Flood was not entirely successful in eradicating the giants and their influences on man.

---

[35] Jeffrey Jerome Cohen, *Of Giants: Sex, Monsters, and the Middle Ages* (London and Minneapolis: University of Minnesota Press), p. xi.
[36] Richard Marsden (ed.), *The Cambridge Old English Reader* (Cambridge: Cambridge University Press, 2004), p. 205.

The Origin of the Giants

In effect, the angels have become *incubi*. This relationship is discussed by St Augustine who argues 'sylvans and fauns, commonly called Incubi, [which] have frequently molested women, sought and obtained from them coition.'[37] This interpretation could have influenced Higden's *Polychronicon* written in the first quarter of the fourteenth century: 'Therefore demon incubi, seeing their advantages and having assumed the shape of men, raped the women, intermingling their seed with the women's seed and immediately vanished into thin air'.[38]

The legend of the giants was popular in the Middle Ages, as well as being a means of explaining astonishing technologies that could not be otherwise explained. Tamar Drukker observes that giants are 'an essential element in foundation myths .... [they] figure as the first traces of human presence in unpopulated regions ... [and] were associated with early history, and ancient ruins and strange phenomena'.[39] There are numerous references to giants in Anglo-Saxon poetry: in *The Ruin* and *Maxims* the building of the ancient city is considered to be 'enta geworc' (*Ruin* l. 2; *Maxims* 2a); *Andreas* (l. 1235) refers to 'enta ærgeweorc' which describe the stone-paved roads.

---

[37] Augustine, *City of God*, Bk15, C.23, cited in Ludovico Maria Sinistrari, *Demoniality*, trans. Isidor Lisieux (Paris: Isidor Liseux, 1879), p. 7.

[38] Quod demones incubi perpendentes assumptis hominum sibi formis cum mixture feminei seminis oppreserunt eiusdem et euanuerunt continuo,' Carley and Crick, 'Constructing Albion's Past', p. 109, cf. Ruth Evans, 'Gigantic Origins', p. 200.

[39] Drukker, 'Thirty-three Murderous Sisters', p. 461.

There are also three references to the work of giants in *Beowulf*. Two of these describe to the encounter with the dragon, most particularly, the dragon's layer (l. 2717) and its treasure (l, 2777). The other instance refers to the giant sword that Beowulf finds when seeking Grendel's mother (l. 1679). Grendel and his mother are associated with 'Cain's kin'; the text describes how:

> fifelcynnes eard
> wonsæli wer weardode hwile,
> siþðan him scyppend forscrifen hæfde
> in Caines cynne. þone cwealm gewræc
> ece drihten, þæs þe he Abel slog;
> ne gefeah he þære fæhðe, ac he hine feor forwræc,
> metod for þy mane, mancynne fram.
> þanon untydras ealle onwocon,
> eotenas ond ylfe ond orcneas,
> swylce gigantas, þa wið gode wunnon
> lange þrage; he him ðæs lean forgeald.

(He had dwelt for a time in misery among the banished monsters, Cain's clan, whom the Creator had outlawed and condemned as outcasts. For the killing of Abel the Eternal Lord had exacted a price: because the Almighty made him anathema and out of the curse of his exile there sprang ogres and elves and evil phantoms and the giants too who strove with God time and again until he gave them their reward.)[40]

While *Beowulf* mentions a direct relationship between Grendel and Cain, the text does not link his ancestry

---

[40] Seamus Heaney (trans.), *Beowulf: Bilingual Edition* (London: Faber and Faber, 2007), ll. 104–15.

The Origin of the Giants

with the Watcher Angels; the sword is the work of giants, and also the work of smiths ('Wundor smiþa geweorc' l. 1681). *Beowulf* later refers to the giants, the Nephilim, being wiped out in the Flood: 'syðþan flod ofsloh gifen geotende giganta cyn' (ll. 1689–90).

The sword that Beowulf discovers on the way to Grendel's mother is directly linked to the teachings of the Watcher Angels called 'giganta geworc' (l. 1562). This concept of the work of giants is repeated in the Anglo-Saxon elegiac poem 'The Wanderer' found in the Exeter Book, observing how

> Yþswa þisne eardgeard ælda Scyppend
> Oþþæt burgwara brehtma lease,
> Eald enta geweorc idlu stodon (*Wan* ll. 85–7).

(The Creator if men thus laid waste this earth/ until deprived of the joy of its inhabitants,/ the ancient work of giants stood empty.)

As mentioned before, the narrator of *Dez Grantz Geanz* is using source material for Geoffrey's *Historia*. The narrator of *Dez Grantz Geanz* justifies the verity of the giants by observing that a man can know this on account of the large bones that can be found across the land. The concept of the heathen giant is a common motif in medieval literature. Often these giants are heathen, and are offered the choice of salvation or returning to their relatives.[41] The idea of a giant girl is also found in the *Liber Monstrorum* written between 650–750:

> And we have heard tell of a certain girl, not yet with swelling breasts, discovered on the western shores of Europe, whom the waves of the sea had brought to land from the Ocean; they marked her size with stones. Indeed fifty feet was the length of her body, and she was seven feet wide between the shoulders.[42]

In the Dutch version of *The Voyage of Brendan*, before setting off on his voyage, Brendan discovers the skull of a giant on the seashore. He is able to speak with it, to offer to baptize it and bring it back to life. The giant refuses resurrection, fearing the second death: 'Supposing I were baptized and yet still unable to resist the Devil's temptations … I would end up in hell once more. Then I should be punished much more severely than now.'[43] As Strijbosch observes 'The giant is a representative of heathens, those who did not know God and are, for that reason reprobated'.[44]

---

[41] Clara Strijbosch, 'The Heathen Giant in the Voyage of St Brendan', *Celtica* 23 (1999): 369–89. Strijbosch notes that the heathen giant episode is unique to the Dutch version of the Brendan legend as a thirteenth century interpolation: It is not found in the Latin or any other vernacular versions.

[42] Andy Orchard, *Pride and Prodigies* (Toronto: University of Toronto Press, 2003), pp. 266–7.

[43] Willem P Gerritsen, 'The Dutch Version' in *The Voyage of Saint Brendan: Representative Versions of the Legend in English Translation*, ed. W.R.J. Barron and Glyn S. Burgess (Exeter: University of Exeter Press, 2005), p.108.

[44] Strijbosch, 'Heathen Giant', p. 388

THE ORIGIN OF THE GIANTS

Later legends of Gog and Magog

It is not clear from the end of *Dez Grantz Geanz* whether Gogmagog survives after the wrestling match or whether he is spared *simply* to recount his story. However, the presence of the giants has been popular in Britain ever since. They often featured in the London pageants: in 1421, processional giants met Henry V when he returned from France; Henry VI was met by a single giant in 1432; and they featured in a pageant to celebrate the visit of the Holy Roman Emperor Charles V in 1522. By 1554, in a pageant celebrating the marriage of Mary and Philip of Spain, the two giants are called *Corineus Britannus* and *Gogmagog Albionus*, they are also seen at the accession of Queen Elizabeth in 1558.[45] Figures of the giants could be seen in the Guildhall in London. The Guildhall, incidentally, was said to have been built on the site of Brutus's Palace, while St Paul's Cathedral was built on the site where Brutus first built a temple dedicated to Diana.[46] The first figures were destroyed in the Great Fire of London in 1666, the second destroyed by rats and damp around 1700. By 1708, new figures stood in the Guildhall, but although they were now known as Gog and Magog, Gog is dressed in a manner associated with

---

[45] Robert Withington, *English Pageantry*, 2 vols. (Cambridge: Harvard University Press, 1918), I, pp. 142, 190.

[46] Thomas Fuller, *The Church History of Britain; From the Birth of Jesus Christ until the Year 1648* (London: Printed for Iohn Williams at the Signe of the Crown in St Paul's Church-yard, 1655), pp. 2-3

the ancient Britons carrying a morning star as a weapon, while Magog wears Roman armour and carries a halberd and shield. Around the same time there were legends of how the *two* giants were brought to London in chains. Sarah Bates claims that they were taken to Brutus's palace (the building that became the Guildhall) where they were chained to the gates to serve as porters.[47] Conversely, Thomas Boreman suggested that the statues celebrate the giants' service:

> Two brave giants ... richly valued their honour, and exerted their strength and force in defence of their liberty and country; so the city of London, by placing these their representatives in their Guildhall, emblematically declare, that they will, like mighty giants, defend the honour of their country, and liberties of this their city.[48]

The eighteenth century figures were unfortunately destroyed during the Blitz in 1940. The statues currently on display were inaugurated in 1953. Gog and Magog still feature in the annual procession for the Lord Mayor's Show in London. Cohen argues that the continued exhibition of the giants is 'a frighteningly

---

[47] Sarah Bates, *The New History of the Trojan Wars and Troy's Destruction in Four Books* (London: Printed for Sarah Bates at the Sun and Bible in Giltspur Street; and James Hodges at the Looking Glass on London Bridge, 1735), p. 144.

[48] Thomas Boreman, *The Gigantick History of the Two Famous Giants, and other Curiosities in Guildhall, London*, 3rd ed. (London: Printed for Thomas Boreman, 1741), p. 53.

public reminder of the monstrous past on which the nation was built'.[49] However, Westwood and Simpson argue that the giants are traditionally viewed as 'Guardians of the City of London and symbols of patriotic pride'.[50]

Conclusion

Lesley Johnson notes that the manuscript *Dez Grantz Geanz* is the only vernacular text in a gathering containing material of strong ecclesiastical and national interest, and Johnson sees significance in that 'a female founder is commemorated amidst chronicles of kings and lists of archbishops and bishops'.[51] And yet, what we see is a series of crimes that pervert the natural order listed against Albina: (attempted) murder, gluttony, lust, sexual gratification with demons, incest between mother and son which and leads to incest between brother and sister. Two and a half centuries later it falls on Brutus and his compatriots to overcome the demon-spawned giants and to repopulate the land with classical, civilised inhabitants. By overcoming the giants, the Trojans ensure their right to habitation.

Throughout the text are a series of ironies: the sisters' father is a king with the power over all kings, and yet he

---

[49] Cohen, *On Giants*, p. 29.
[50] Jennifer Westwood and Jacqueline Simpson, *The Lore of the Land* (London: Penguin Books, 2005), p. 468.
[51] Johnson, 'Return to Albion', p. 40.

has no control over his daughters; their father is king because of his virtue. The daughters are exiled because of their deceit; they desire mastery over their husbands, and yet their fate is decided by their father who sides with their husbands, and even then they do not challenge his authority. Consequently, the sisters are figures of defiance rather than authority themselves. Their planned crimes lead to their exile in a boat over which they have no control. Once on the island, instead of enjoying a regal life of comfort, they are forced to hunt their own food; but they have to do this without the accessories for noble hunting and are forced to fashion makeshift traps. They were married to noble kings, but they mate with incubi, and while they were loath to be dominated by their husbands, it seems that the incubi are able to assert their authority with comparative ease. Even though Albina establishes her claim on the land by giving it her name, she is not the founder of a nation, but the matriarch of a race of demonic, incestuous giants. The text notes that the Britons 'removed the first name' (*le premier noun osterent* l. 555), and the honour of naming the land is given to Brutus 'wanted to be remembered for ever for giving them [his followers] his name'. Finally, while Gogmagog is clearly a figure of masculine monstrosity, hideous to look at (*A regarder hidous*, l. 457) the planned actions of Albina and her sisters are equally monstrous. Thus, as Julia Marvin argues, 'it is a cautionary tale about the use and abuse of lineage and power'. She continues that 'The conformity of the youngest sister is rewarded and the transgressions of the others punished and quarantined, exiled beyond the boundaries of the known world.'[52]

In contrast, Brutus, who, according to the prophecy, killed both his mother and his father, undertakes a purgatorial voyage around the Mediterranean and finally atones for his guilt by the extermination of the giants.

Dez Grantz Geanz was widely disseminated in the vernacular at a time when writing histories was much more common in Latin. Because of its popularity, it makes a significant contribution to the development of English cultural identity. In historical terms, it seeks to reinforce the link to a Trojan ancestry as presented by Nennius and advanced by Geoffrey and Wace. In literary terms, it is one of the few epic verse poems written in England in the fourteenth century and provides a link between the literary chronicles and the development of Romance Poetry. It is also an early example of a morality tale, which highlights the sins of pride, gluttony and lechery, and thus prepares the way for later texts such as William Langland's *Piers Plowman*.

---

[52] Julia Marvin, 'Albine and Isabelle', p 145.

J.S. Mackley

Appendix 1

This appendix contains the end of chapter 20 and the whole of chapter 21 from Geoffrey of Monmouth's, *Historia Regum Britanniae*.

(20) Favourable winds brought him to the promised isle, where he came ashore at Totnes.

(21) The island was at that time called Albion; it had no inhabitants save for a few giants. The choice position of this pleasant land, its numerous rivers, good for fishing and its woods led Brutus and his companions to want to settle there. After exploring its various territories and driving off to mountain caves any giants they came upon, they portioned out the land, at their leader's invitation and they began to till the fields and build homes so that, in a short time, the country appeared to have been occupied for many years. Brutus named the island Britain after himself and called his followers Britons. He wanted to be remembered forever for giving them his name. For this reason the language of his people, previously known as Trojan or 'Crooked Greek', was henceforth called British. Corineus followed his leader's example by simply calling the area of the kingdom allotted to him Corinea and his people Corineians, after himself. He could have had his pick of the provinces before any other settler, but he preferred the region now called Cornwall, either after Britain's horn or through a corruption of the name Corineia. He

The Origin of the Giants

loved to fight giants, and there were more of them to be found there than in any other of the districts divided amongst his companions. One of these Cornish giants was a monster called Goemagog, twelve cubits tall and so strong he could loosen and uproot an oak tree as if it were a twig of hazel. One day when Brutus was holding a feast for the gods at the port where he had landed, Goemagog arrived with twenty giants and inflicted terrible carnage on the Britons. Eventually, as more Britons flocked to their aid, they beat the giants and killed them all except Goemagog. Brutus had ordered that his life be spared because he wanted to see him wrestle with Corineus, who was always most eager to fight giants. Overjoyed, Corineus hitched up his tunic, threw his weapons aside and challenged the giant to wrestle. The bout began, both Corineus and the giant closing to encircle each other with their arms, whilst their panting breath disturbed the air. Goemagog swiftly gripped Corineus with all his strength and broke three of his ribs, two on the right side and one on the left. This goaded Corineus to fury and, summoning all his might, he lifted the giant on his shoulders and ran to the nearby shore as fast as his burden would allow. Coming to the edge of a high cliff, he hurled over the fearful monster he bore on his shoulders, casting him into the sea. As he fell down the rocky crag, the giant was torn into a thousand pieces and stained the sea red with his blood. The place took its name from the giants' plunge and is still called Goemagog's Leap.

Appendix 2

Extract from the First Book of Enoch

The First Book of Enoch, which describes the Watcher Angels, is a *pseudepigraphical* legend: the word taken from the Greek literally means 'falsely attributed' and refers to texts written at the same time as books of the Bible, but which were attributed to authors who did not write them.

> It happened that there were born unto them [the children of men] handsome and beautiful; daughters. And the angels, the children of heaven, saw them and desired them; and they said to one another, 'Come, let us choose wives for ourselves and from among the daughters of men and beget us children.' ... And they took wives unto themselves, and everyone (respectively) chose one woman for himself, and they began to go unto them. And they taught them magical medicine, incantations, the cutting of roots, and taught them (about) plants. And the women became pregnant and gave birth to great giants whose heights were three hundred cubits. These (giants) consumed the produce of all the peoples until the people detested feeding them. So the giants turned against (the people) in order to eat them. And they began to sin against birds, wild beasts, reptiles, and fish. And their flesh was devoured the one by the other, and they drank blood. (1 Enoch 6: 1, 2; 7: 1–5).[53]

---

[53] James H Charlesworth (ed.) *The Old Testament Pseudepigrapha* (New York and London: Doubleday, 1983): 13–89, pp. 15–16. A cubit is

THE ORIGIN OF THE GIANTS

Translator's note:

This is a literal – line by line – translation, rather than a literary translation. The main aim has been to convey the meaning of the Anglo-Norman and to keep the text to the same line as the original.

{ has been used when it has been necessary to convey the meaning over two or more lines

[ ] has been used to add words for clarity.

The author frequently switches from past to present tense, and back again. Where possible, we have followed the author.

---

approximately 45cm, so these giants would have been 135 metres tall. Noah's ark is also measured as 300 cubits long (Genesis 6:15).

The Origin of the Giants:
The First Settlers of Albion

Dez Grantz Geanz

Ci put hom saver coment
E quant e de quele gent
Les grantz geantz primes vindrent
Qi Engletere primes tindrent,[54]
Qe primes fu nomé Albion,
E qe primes mist le noum.
Ore escotez peniblement,
E l'em vous dirra brevement
Des geanz tote la soume,
Cum jeo l'oy de un sage home   10
Qi bien saveit les escriptures
Des auncienes aventures.[55]
Aprés le comensement
Del mound, treis mil e nef cent
E sessante e diz anz,
En Grece estoit un roy pussanz,
Qi tant fu pruz e noble e fier
Qe sur touz reys aveit poer.
Reyne avoit bele e gente
En qi engendra filez trente,   20
Forment beles, qe tant crurent,
E norries ensemble furent.
Pere e mere furent granz,
Ausi devindrent les enfanz.
Lur nouns ne vous say cunter,
Unkes ne les oy nomer,
Fors cele qu estoit eynez,
Qe mult fu bele e haut levez ;

---

[54] Cf. Wace's *Brut*, ll. 1–4.
[55] Cf. ll. 559–60 below.

THE ORIGIN OF THE GIANTS

Here one can know how
And when and from which race
The great giants first came
Who first held England
And which first was called Albion
And who first gave it its name.
Now listen carefully
And you will be told briefly
All that is to be known about the giants
As I heard it from a wise man
Who was very familiar with the writings
About happenings in olden times.
{Three thousand nine hundred
{And seventy years
{After the beginning of the world
There was in Greece a powerful king
Who was so wise and noble and proud
That he had power over all the other kings.
He had a queen, beautiful and fair
By whom he fathered thirty daughters
Very beautiful, who all grew [up],
And they were nurtured together.
Father and mother were big
And so the children [grew big] too.
I could not tell you their names,
I never heard them named
Apart from the one who was the eldest
Who was very beautiful and proud;[56]

---

[56] 'haut levez' may refer to her upbringing, her pride or her height.

Mult estoit bele meschine:
Cele fu nomez Albine.   30
E quant totes furent de age,
A grant roys de haut parage
Totes les fillez donerent,
E as haut roys marierent.
Chescune out roy e fu reyne,
Mes par orgoil de lur meyme
E par fierté e grant rage
Purpenserent grant outrage,
Par unt grant damage avoient.
Mes rien adonkes ne quidoient   40
Qe rien leur pout a mal turner
Ceo q'il avoient en penser.
Mes tost aprés se assemblerent,
E coyment se conselerent,
E si unt entre eux ordiné
Qe nule ne soit si assoté
De suffrir en nule guise
De estre en autri danger mise,
Ne de seignur, ne de veisin,
Ne de frere, ne de cosin,   50
Ne nomément de sun barun.
'Mes touz jours en subjection
Ci li tegnez en danger,[57]
Si averez tut vostre voler.'
Fillez erent au roy de pris
Qi a nuli ne fut souzmis ;

---

[57] Lit. 'power'.

4

THE ORIGIN OF THE GIANTS

She was a very beautiful girl:
Her name was Albine.
And when they all came of age
{They gave all their daughters
{To kings of noble lineage
And married them to important kings.
Each one had her king and was a queen,
But through their own pride
And through arrogance and great madness
They plotted a great wicked deed,
Through which they [came to] great harm.
But they did not think at that time
That anything could go wrong
With that which they had in mind.
But soon afterwards they got together,
And quietly deliberated among themselves,
And so they have decided among themselves
That no-one [of them] should be so foolish
As to suffer in any form
To be subject to the authority of another
Neither of a lord, nor a neighbour,
Nor of a brother, nor a cousin,
Nor especially of her lord.
{'But every day you would hold them
{Under [your] control, under [your] authority,
If you all had your free will.'
They were daughters of a worthy king
Who was subject to no-one.

Ne ne voleient eles estre,
Nule ne voleit aver mestre,
Ne estre souz nuli destresce ;
Mes tutdis estre mestresce   60
De sun seignur e quant q'il out.
A chescune cel conseil plout.
Si lur seignurs a lur voler
Ne se voleient obeier
De fere tote lur volunté
De quant q'il unt en pensé,
Entre eux issint asseurerent
E par lur feiz affermerent
Qe chescune, tut en un jour,
Oscireit mesme sun seignur,   70
Privément entre ces braz,
Quant meux quide aver solaz.
Un certein jour assignerent
A faire cum purparlerent.
Totes unt ceo en voluntez
Fors qe soulement le puisnez ;
Cele ne voleit mespresndre rien
Vers sun seignur, q'ele eime bien.
Quant tut lur conseil unt finé,
En lur pays sunt returnez.   80
Ceste chose purparlee
Rien ne plout a la puisné
Qe sun seignur atant eyme
Cum ele fet sun cors demeine.
Ele ne voleit a nul feur
Damage veer de sun seignur ;

THE ORIGIN OF THE GIANTS

Neither did they wish to be [the subjects of anyone]
None of them wanted to have a master
Nor to be under anyone's constraint;
But always to be mistress
Of her lord and all he possessed.
This scheme pleased them all.
{If their lords did not wish
{To submit to their will
[And] to do all that they wished
To the extent that they have in mind
Accordingly they committed themselves
And affirmed under oath
That each one, all on one day,
Would herself kill her lord
In private in her arms
Where he would most expect to find comfort.
They designated a particular day
To do as they [had] discussed.
They all have the will to do this
Except only for the youngest one;
She wished to do no wrong
To her lord, whom she loved greatly.
When they have finished all their discussions
They have [all] gone back to their countries.
{Nothing about that thing [that they had] talked about
{Pleased the youngest one
Who loves her lord as much
As she [loves] herself
She did not wish at any cost
To see any harm [come] to her lord;

Mes quant furent a parlement,
Nes osa contredire nien ;
Kar, si ele ust rien contredist,
Murdré la usseit sanz respit.   90
Dieu li amoit qe lors se tint.
Si tost cum pout al hostel vint ;
Quant vist sun mari sun doel crust ;
E quant sun seignur le aperceust
Q'ele fesoit mourne semblant,
Si l'a demandé meintenant
Pur quei ele estoit dolent.
E la dame, qe mult ert gent,
A piez sun seignur descendi,
En plorant li cria merci.   100
De sun trespaz merci cria
E de la trayson li counta,
Coment ses soers, a mult grant tort,
Li fesoient jurer sa mort,
La ou de ceo n'avoit talent.
E sun seignur hastivement
La prist mult tost entre ces braz,
La beise, e fist greignour solaz
Qe fait li avoit unques mes.
'Dame,' fait il, 'tenez en pes,   110
E lessez passer la dolour.'
L'endemain, a point de jour,
Se apparila pur tost aler

The Origin of the Giants

But when they were in their discussions
She dared not gainsay anything;
For, if she had gainsaid anything
They would have murdered her without delay.
God loved her so she restrained herself then
As soon as she could she went home;
When she saw her husband her grief increased
And when her lord noticed
That she seemed to be sad
He asked her immediately
Why she was suffering.
And the lady, who was very noble,
Knelt down at his feet
In tears she begged for his forgiveness.
For her sin she begged forgiveness
And told him about the betrayal
How her sisters, very much in the wrong,
Made her swear his death
When she had no desire.
And her lord promptly
Took her very quickly into his arms,
Kisses her and gave her greater comfort
Than he had ever done before.
'My lady', says he, 'Be at peace,
And let the pain ease.'
The following day, at day-break,
He got dressed to go early

A sun pere, ou li parler,
E a sa femme dist ensi
Q'ele seit preste de aler ou li.
Ne demorra pas grant pece,
Vers sun pere, roy de Grece,
Ambdeux lur voie tindrent.
Tant errerent q'il vindrent;   120
Mult sunt a roy tres bien venuz,
E tut si cum fust avenuz
De ses fillez li unt contee.
E li roy fust tut espounté
De ceo qe sa fille li dist.
Brefs e lettres escrivere fist :
Ses filles manda erraument
Qe a li viegnent hastivemen[t].
E quant furent touz assemblé,
Li roy les ad aresonee   130
De la mort e la trayson
Qe chescune de sun barun,
Par grant malice, avoit purveu,
Dunt deshonur lur est acreu.
Les dames sunt touz espontez
De ceo q'eles sunt acoupez
De la trayson dunt sunt rettez,
Dunt ja ne serrunt aquitez ;
Mes chescune, a sun poer,
Se veut defendre par jurer.   140
Mes rien ne vaut le contredire,

The Origin of the Giants

To her father, to speak with him
And so he told his wife
To get ready to go with him.
It was not a great distance[58]
To her father, the King of Greece,
Both of them went on their way.
They travelled so quickly that they [soon] arrived;
They reached the king safe and sound
And as soon as they arrived
They told him about his daughters.
And the king was quite horrified
By what his daughter told him.
He had documents and letters written:
He ordered his daughters forthwith
To come to him promptly.
And when they were all assembled,
The king addressed them
About the death and betrayal
{That each one [of his daughters] had plotted
{Against her lord, through great evil intent,
Which has brought shame upon them.
The ladies are quite terrified
At that of which they are accused
At the betrayal for which they are blamed
For which they will never be acquitted;
But each one as far as possible,
Wants to defend herself under oath.
But their denial is worth nothing,

---

[58] Lit 'A long time'

Car li roy out si grant ire
Qe touz les veut mettre a mort
Pur lur malice e pur lur tort.
Lur pere, qi out ire grant,
Tant les ala aresonant
E tant a les ad examiné
Qe rien ne pout estre celé
De ceo qe purveu avoient
Quant a lur conseil estoient.   150
Par lur pere, qe fu coynte,
Fust chescune la ateinte
De cele malice desraee ;
Fors soulement la puisnee,
Qe tut counta a sun seignur,
Qi puis la tint a grant honur.
    Quant chescune fu ateinte
De la dolerouse pleinte,
Touz furent a dolour pris
Par lur pere e lur mariz.   160
En forte prison furent botez
Par lur mauveise iniquitez.
Grant penance la suffrirent,
E juyse attendirent
Ci la qe par commun assent
Fust ordiné lur jugement.
Mes les juges, qi furunt sage,
Pur l'onur de lur parage,
C'est a saver de lur pere,
Ausi de lur bone mere,   170

The Origin of the Giants

For the king was so very angry
That he wants to put them all to death
For their wickedness and their wrongdoing.
Their father, who was exceedingly angry,
Went about berating them so much
And questioned them so much
That nothing could be concealed
Of what they had plotted
When they were at their conclave.
By their father, who was astute,
Each one was convicted
Of this unrighteous malice
Except alone for the youngest,
Who told everything to her lord,
Who then held her in great esteem.
When each one [of the daughters] was confronted
With the painful accusation,
All were taken with regret
By their father and their husbands.
Into a secure prison they were thrust
Because of their evil crime.
They endured severe punishment there
And awaited judgment
Until [by] common agreement
Their sentence was passed.
But the judges, who were wise,
In honour of their lineage,
Namely that of their father,
And also their good mother,

Qe si noble gent estoient
Qe partut l'empire avoient,
E pur l'onur de lur barons,
Qi tindrent riche regions,
Unt agardé qe a dreit ne a tort[59]
Ne deivent suffrir vile mort.
Mes par commun assentement
Fu ordiné par jugement
Qe totes seient exilez
Hors du pais ou furent nez   180
A touz jours, sanz repeirer.
Cest jugement estuet suffrir,
Ou seit envys, ou seit a gré :
Hom dist qe force pest le pré!
A grant dolour e sanz resort
Menez furent a un port
Ben pres d'illoek a la mer.
Ou ceo fu ne vous sai counter,
Mes qe totez furent prises
E puis en une nef mises,   190
Qe estoit forte e grande,
Sanz governail e sanz viande
Mes nul n'avoit de eux pité
Pur lur grant iniquité
Q'entre eux fut purparlé.
En la mer la nef botirent;

---

[59] 'Agardé' OF *esgarder* – a legal term 'to decide judicially'.

The Origin of the Giants

Who were such noble folk
That they ruled everywhere,
And for the honour of their lords,
Who ruled over rich areas,
[They] have decreed that [whether they are] in the right or in the wrong
They must not suffer a base death.
But by common assent
It was decreed in the judgment
That they should all be exiled
From the country where they were born
For ever, without return.
This judgment was to be endured,
Whether they liked it or not[60]
It is said that might is right!
With great sorrow and without resource
They were taken to a port
Very close to the sea.
Where this was, I could not say,
Only that they were all taken
And then put in a ship,
Which was big and strong,
Without steering and without food
But no-one had pity on them
Because of their great wickedness
Which they had plotted amongst themselves.
They pushed off into the sea;

---

[60] Lit: 'Either willingly or unwillingly'.

Les undes la nef chacerent
En grant peril, sa e la;
De la tere les esloigna.   200
En grant dolour sunt ore mis
Quant exilez sunt de lur pais,
Dunt furent riche reignez –
Ore sunt il povere begynes.[61]
Ne scevunt quele part devendrunt,
Si morz ou vives eschaperunt.

    Cestes dames unt grant peine :
Aventure la nief meine,
Les grant venz par mer la chacent,
E les undes la manacent ;   210
Mes rien tant de mal ne lur fet
Cum la famine qe lur crest,
Car rien n'avoient a manger;
Mes pur le peril de la mer
Pitousement waymenterent,
E la famine ublierent.
De tote part sunt turmenté,
Morir voleient de bon gré.
Chescune grant dolur attent,

---

[61] The lay sisterhood of the Beguines are women who lived in monastic communities and devoted themselves to prayer without taking religious vows, sometimes associated with beggars. For further discussion see Walter Simons, *Cities of Ladies: Beguine Communities in the Medieval Low Countries, 1200-1565* (Philadelphia: University of Pennsylvania Press, 2003); Laura Swan, *The Wisdom of the Beguines: The Forgotten Story of a Medieval Women's Movement* (New York: BlueBridge, 2014)

The Origin of the Giants

The waves chased the ship
Into great danger, here and there;
And [the ship] took them away from the land.
They now suffer a great sadness
When they are exiled from their country,
Of which they were rich queens -
Now they are poor beggars
They do not know where they will arrive,
[Nor] whether they will come out dead or alive.
      These ladies endure great suffering:
Destiny leads the ship,
The strong winds drive her across the sea,
And the waves threaten her;
But nothing hurts them so much
As the hunger which grows within them
For they had nothing to eat;
But because of the danger of the sea
They lamented piteously,
And forgot [about] the[ir] hunger.
They are tormented from every side,
They would willingly have died.[62]
Each one suffered great sadness,

---

[62] Lit: 'They wanted to die willingly'.

Car en la mer leva un vent 220
Qe la fist crestre e lever
E les granz undes reverser;
E tressailler fist la nief amount,
E pus flotir a plus parfount ;
E tant la turna envirun
Qe les dames en paumesun
Fesoit chaier e giser
Par .iii. jours e .iii. nuytz enter,
Qe de rien ne se moverent,
Mes tutdiz en trauns giserent. 230
Endementers les enporte
La tempeste qe fu forte,
E les chace par grant travail
Qe pres sunt venuz a un rivail.
    Quant fu cessé la tempeste
–Cum nous trovoms en la geste–
Le tens devint cler e swef,
E tant par west chace la nef
Qe la tere est hurté
Qe Engletere est ore nomé ; 240
Mes en ceo tens sanz noun estoit,
Pur ceo qe nul home n'i manoit.
Quant la mer retrete fust,
La nef a secke tere geust.
Les dames tost esveillerent,

The Origin of the Giants

For the wind rose in the sea
Which made it heave and swell
And [made] the big waves turn over;
And made the ship leap on the crest
And then fall down at the trough;
And turned it around so much
{That it made the ladies
{Fall into a swoon and lie down
For three [whole] days and three whole nights,
[So that] they did not move at all,
But all the time lay in a coma.
{Meanwhile the storm, which was strong,
{Carries them away,
And blows them along with great turmoil
So that they have come close to a shore.
    When the storm had ceased
– As we discover in the chronicle –
The weather became clear and calm,
And drives the ship so far west
That they strike the land,[63]
Which is now called England;
But at that time was without name,
For the reason that no man lived there.
When the tide had gone out
The ship rested on dry ground.
The ladies soon woke up,

---

[63] Lit: 'The land is struck'.

E lur testes susleverent.
Grant joie trestotes eurent
Qe si pres de tere furent.
Tantost de la nef issirent,
Ou tres malveis sojour firent ;[64]   250
Mes cele soer qe fu eyné
Avant totes se est hasté
Tut premereine en saillant,
La terre prist tut en estant.
Cele qe fu nomee Albine
De la terre prist seysine,
E les autres hors saillerent
De la nef, qe febles erent
Pur la dolour e le juner
Q'il avoient en la mer.   260
Chescune a terre se assist ;
Lur grant famine les reprist,
Qe tut fust ublié devant
Pur la tempeste qe fu grant.
Feym avoient a demesure,
D'autre rien n'avoient cure
Mes qu'il ussunt a manger,
Mes nel savoient ou trover
Mes par grant necesseté
Les herbes crues unt mangé   270
Dunt grant plenté i troverent,
E des fruits qe es arbes erent.
Glens, chasteins e allies

---

[64] ll. 247–49, cf. *Brut* 1057–9.

THE ORIGIN OF THE GIANTS

And raised their heads.
They all rejoiced greatly.
[To discover] that they were so close to land.
They got out of the boat immediately,
Where they had [had] a very unpleasant stay;
But that sister who was the eldest
Hurried out before them all
The very first on jumping out,
She took [control of] the land as she stood up
She who was named Albine
Took possession of the land,
{And the others, who were weak
{Through the suffering and lack of food
{That they had [endured] on the sea,
{Jumped out of the ship.
Each one sat down on the ground;
Their great hunger took hold of them again,
So that everything before was forgotten
About the storm that was great.
They were exceedingly hungry,
They cared about nothing else
Other than that they might have [something] to eat,
But they did not know where to find [any]
But through great necessity
They have eaten raw plants
Which they found in abundance
And the fruits which were on the trees.
Acorns, chestnuts and beam-tree berries

Sustinoient bien lur vies,
E des espines les purneles,
Botouns de haie, e meeles,
Peires, poumes q'eles troverent,
Autre viannde ne mangerent.
Totes sunt en grant pensé
Ne scevent ou sunt arivé   280
Ne coment ad noun la terre.
Ou seit de pes, ou seit de guerre,
La lur covent sojour fere,
N'estuet aillours autre quere.
   Quant revigurez estoient
De la dolur q'il avoient,
Amont alerent en la terre
Per espier e enquere
Quele gent i habitoient
E quele vie demenoient.   290
En la terre tant alerent
Qe par mi tut la cercherent.
Rien ne troverent humeine
En boscage, ne en pleine,
Ne en valey, ne sur mont,
Qe haut e bas illoqes sunt.
Home ne femme ne troverent,[65]
Dunt grantment s'esmerveillerent ;
Ne nul rien unt aperceu

---

[65] Cf. *Brut*, l. 622

The Origin of the Giants

Sustained their lives well,
And the sloes from the thorn,
Fruits of the hawthorn, and medlars[66]
Pears, apples, which they found
They did not eat [any] other food.
They are very anxious,
They do not know where they have arrived
Nor what the land's name is.
Whether it was in peace or at war,
It suited them to sojourn there,
There was nowhere else to go.

When they were reinvigorated
From the suffering they had [endured],
They went up into the country
To search and discover
What people lived there
And what [sort of] life they lived.
They travelled so far inland
And looked everywhere[67]
They found nothing human
In the woodland, nor on the plain,
Nor in the valley[s], nor on the hill[s],
Which are there, high and low.
They found neither man nor woman,
At which they wondered greatly;
Nor did they notice anything

---

[66] A fruit like a cross between an apple and a rosehip, indigenous to the lands of southwest Asia and also south eastern Europe. Chaucer uses it as a symbol of prostitution and premature decay.

[67] Lit 'They had looked for it [people] among everything'.

Qe unques gent i fust venu.　　　　　　　　　　300
Mes bele forest e boscage
E meinte beste sauvage
I troverent a grant fuysun,
E grant plenté de oyseloun
Sur terre, e en rivers
Qe de pesson sunt pleners;
E de encoste praieries
Delitablement flories.
E les oyseux, qe sunt sauvages,
Chaunterent haut en les boscages, [68]　　　310
Qe les ad mis en grant confort.
Mes quant veiient qe par nul sort
Ne purrount ja aver poer
De lur pais recoverer,
Mes bien scevent e certeinz sunt
Qe la terre qe trové unt
Unqes ne fu enhabitee
Par nul home de mere nee
– Ceo unt il trové tut apert
Qe titdis ad esté desert –　　　　　　　　　　320
Adonk dist la soer eynnee,
Qe estoit Albine nomee :
'Trestotez sumes exilez
De la terre ou fumes neez ;
Totes savez la desserte
Par unt nous avint la perte
Qe mes nen ert restorré.

---

[68] ll. 301–10 is taken from chapters 5 and 21 of Geoffrey's *Historia*.

The Origin of the Giants

[To suggest] that people had ever been there.
But beautiful forest and woodland
And many a wild animal
They found there in great profusion,
And game-birds aplenty
On [the] land and in [the] rivers
Which are abundant with fish;
And meadows alongside
Delightfully laden with flowers.
And the birds, which are wild,
Sang loudly in the woods,
Which comforted them greatly.
But when they see that by no happenstance
Will they ever have the possibility
To regain their country
But they know well and are certain
That the land that they have found
Had never been inhabited
By no man born of a mother
– This they have found quite obvious
That it has always been uninhabited –
Then said the eldest sister,
Who was called Albine:
'We are completely exiled
From the land where we were born;
You all know of the guilt
Through which the loss came about
That will never be restored.

Tiele est nostre destinee ;
Mes fortune nous ad grantee
Ceste terre, ou avowé 330
Estre dei, e cheveteine,
Car jeo fu la premereine
Q'en la terre prist seysine,[69]
Al issir de la marine.
Si nule veut contredire
Rien qe touche la matire,
Meintenant le mostre a mei
Pur quey estre ne le dei.'
Communement li unt grantee
Q'ele seit lur avowee.[70] 340

    Dunqes dit la dame Albine :
'La terre avomes encline,
Dunt ne savoms le noun dire,
Ne si unques avoit sire.
Pur ceo de moi, qe su feffee,
Deit la terre estre nomee.
Albine est mon propre noun,
Dunt serra nomé Albion ;[71]
Remembrance serra tutdis. 350
Ci nous covent tutdis maner,
N'avoms cure aillours aler,
La terre est pleine de touz biens,
Mes qe viande n'i faut riens.'

---

[69] Feudal term
[70] ll. 330, 340 'Avowé' refers to a feudal lord, although in these lines the term refers to a woman.
[71] ll. 345–49 cf. Geoffrey, *Historia*, ch 21 and Wace, *Brut*, ll. 1207–12.

The Origin of the Giants

Such is our destiny;
But fortune has given us
{This land, where I should be overlord
{And mistress
For I was the very first
Who took possession of the land,
When coming off the sea.
If anyone wishes to gainsay
Anything appertaining to this matter,
[She should] prove to me now
Why I have no right to be so.'
Unanimously they have acknowledged
That she should be their overlord.
    Then the lady Albine said:
'We have won over the land
Of which we do not know how to say the name
Nor if it ever had a lord.
{For this reason the land must be named
{After me, as the feoffee.
Albine is my name
Therefore it will be called Albion;
{People will remember us
{In this country always.
It suits us to remain always
We have no intention to go elsewhere
The land is full of all produce,
With the exception of meat we want for nothing there.'[72]

---

[72] Lit: 'there is nothing missing'.

Mult unt desir d'avoir viande
Tel cum lur quer demaunde.
Bestes veient a grant plenté,
E oyseloun, dunt sunt tempté ;
Volenters les mangereient
Si entre meins les avereint   360
Totes furent en grant pensé
Coment pussent a volunté
Aver beste ou oyseloun,
Dunt il avoit grant fuysoun.
Assez savoient de chacer
Quant avoient lige poer,
E de boys e de rivere
Bien savoient la manere ;
Mes lors n'avoient nule rien,
Ark ne sete, faucon ni chien   370
Dunt preissent oysel ne beste
Qe manger pussent a feste.
Coyntes e engynouses erent,
Estreitement se purpenserent,
Dunt, par grant avisement,
Engyns fesoient plus de cent.
Des verges firent hardilouns
Dunt il pristerent veneisouns ;
Tripecchés firent de fusseux
Dunt pristerent le oyseux ;   380
Divers engyns sovent firent,
E si coyntement tendirent,

The Origin of the Giants

They have a great desire for meat
Such as their heart longs for
They see animals in great numbers,
And birds, by which they are tempted;
They would like to eat them
If they could get hold of them.
They all gave a great deal of thought
[To] how they could at will
Have animals or birds[73]
Of which there was a great abundance.
They knew enough about hunting
[From] when they had feudal power,
{And they were very familiar
{With the nature of woods and rivers:
But there they had nothing at all,
Bow nor arrow, falcon nor dog,
With which they could capture bird or beast
That they could eat with pleasure.
They were clever and ingenious,
They reflected earnestly,
As a result of which, after great consideration,[74]
They made more than a hundred contrivances.
From switches they made snares
In which they caught game;
They made bird-snares from sticks of wood
In which they caught the birds;
All sorts of contraptions they often made
And set them so cleverly,

---

[73] Little bird, gosling, game-bird
[74] Lit: 'From which, as a result of great deliberation'

Dunt les bestes decevoient
E oyselouns assez pernoient.
Quant urent pris a volunté
La veneisoun unt escorché ;
Des cayllous unt feu alumé
Busche avoient a plenté ;
En quirs les bestes quisserent,
E par les breses rostirent   390
La veneison e les oyseux
Qe pris avoient, bons e beaux ;
Dunt mult leement se peurent,
De ewe de fontayne beurent.
Tiele vie tant sustindrent
Qe lur forces tut revindrent,
E bien furent reviguree
Du mal qe avoient enduré.

    Quant char e sanc reperneient,
Grosses e grasses deveneient.   400
La chaline de nature
Les somount a desmesure
Par desir de lecherie
D'avoir humeine cumpanie–
De ceo sunt mult sovent tempté.
Ceo aperceurent li malfee
Qe sunt apellez Incubi.
Ceo sunt espiritz, jeo vous di,
Qe tiel poer lors avoient :

The Origin of the Giants

[That] by this means they deceived the animals
And caught enough birds.
When they had caught enough, [75]
They have skinned the game;
With stones they have lit a fire,
They had plenty of wood;
They cooked the animals in their skins,
And on the embers they roasted
The game and the birds
That they had caught, fine and good;
Which they consumed very gladly
And drank water from the fountain.
They sustained such a way of life so well,
That their strength returned completely,
And they were well reinvigorated
From the suffering that they had endured.
        When they had recovered flesh and blood
They became big and fat.
Natural lust[76]
Arouses them disproportionately,
Through desire of lechery,
To have carnal intercourse–
They are often tempted by this.
{The demons, which are called Incubi,
{Noticed this.
These are spirits, I am telling you,
Who then had such great power:

---

[75] Lit: 'at will'
[76] Lit: 'heat'

Humeine forme pernoient,　　　　　　　　410
Oveqes ceo la nature ;
Ou femmes firent mixture ;
Quant en delit[77] les troverent
En cel point les pargiserent,
Sovent enfanz engenarerent,
E tost aprés s'envanerent.
A les dames avint ensi ;
Quant lur delit les assailly
Mult prest esteient li malfee
De parempler lur volunté　　　　　　　　420
En la forme avant dite.
Ne fu grande ne petite
Qe ne fu prise de un malfee ;
E la furent engendré
Enfaunz qi geaunz devindrent,
E aprés la terre tindrent.
Tut lur delit acumplirent ;
Mes les dames rien ne virent
Ceux qi pargieu les avoient,
Mes qe soulement sentoient　　　　　　　430
Come femme deit home fere
Quant s'entremet de tiel afere.
E quant furent de meur age,
Les enfanz, par grant outrage,
En lur meres engendrerent
Filz e filles qe grantz erent.
Les soers de freres conceurent

---

[77] Pleasure, but in a negative sense

The Origin of the Giants

They took on human form,
[And] with that [human] nature;
They had sexual intercourse with women;
When they found them with their desire aroused
They lay with them at this moment,
Often they fathered children,
And soon afterwards they disappeared.
It happened thus to the ladies;
When their desire assailed them
The demons were very ready
To fulfil their wish
In the aforesaid manner.
There was neither a big one nor a small one
Who was not taken by an evil spirit;
And in that way were fathered
Children who became giants,
And afterwards ruled the land.
They all fulfilled their desire;
But the ladies did not see at all
Those who had violated them in sexual intercourse,
But [they] felt only
Like a woman is supposed to do
When she gets involved in such matters.
And when they reached maturity
The children, in [acts of] great transgression,
Fathered in their mothers
Sons and daughters who were big.
The sisters produced, by the brothers,

Filz e filles qe mult crurent ;
Grantz gentz de cors devenoient,
E grant force en eux avoient. 440
Grantz erent a desmesure
E de cors e d'estature.
Ceo puet home mult ben sa[ver]
Par les grantz os qu hom puet tro[ver]
En mult des leus de la terre,
Qe vodra cercher e enquere.
Oppelannd e en cité
Puet hom trover a grant plent[é]
Dentz, jambes e costez,
E quisses de quatre peez ; 450
Espaudles ad hom bien veu
Ausi large cum un escu ;
Dunt mult de gent sunt en eswer
Si puet estre faus ou veir,
Si unqes furent tieles gentz
Qi portassent tiel ossementz.
A regarder hidous erent,
Car malfez les engendrerent.
Des deables furent engendrez,
E les meres dunt furent nez 460
Furent grandes e mult corsues,
De forte gent furent venues.
Par reson si deivent estre
Les enfanz qi deivent nestre
De tiele gent cum cil erent

The Origin of the Giants

Sons and daughters who grew very big;
They became great giants in size[78]
And had great intrinsic strength.
They were excessively big
Both in body and in height.
This can easily be verified
From the big bones that can be found
In many places in the land,
[By] anyone who wishes to look and investigate.
In the country and in the town
One can find in great profusion
Teeth, legs and ribs,
And thigh [bones] four feet long;
One has seen clearly shoulder [blades]
As wide as a shield;
About [this] many people are disputing
Whether it can be true or false,
Whether such people ever existed
Who might have had such bones.
They were hideous to look at,
Because demons [had] fathered them.
They were fathered by devils,
And the mothers who gave birth to them
Were big and very stout,
They had come from strong stock.
{[There was] a reason [for the fact] that
{The giants fathered children [like this]
{[Since they] were to be born

---

[78] Lit: 'In body'.

Qe les geaunz engendrerent.
    Cele gent de faierie
Mult grantment se multiplie ;
Par la terre se partirent
E caves en terre firent :   470
Grant murs entour funt lever
E des fossés envirouner ;
Sur montaines herbergerent
Ou meux estre en seur quiderent.
En mult des leus unkore i pierent
Les grant murs qe cil leverent,
Mes mult sunt ore abessee
Par tenpeste e par orree.
Cele gent la terre tindrent
Ci la qe les Bretons vindrent.   480
Ceo fu avant qe Dieu fu nee,
Cum par acounte ai trovee,
Mil cent aunz e trente sis,
De ceo soiez certein tutdis.
    Del tens qe les dames vindrent
Qe primes la terre tindrent,
Jeques au tens qe Brutus vint
E la terre a force tint,
E le noun Albion osta,
E pus Bretayne la noma,   490
Si cum la cronike counte
Deux centz e sessaunte amounte ;
Tant de tens, ceo fet a crere,
Les geaunz tindrent la terre.

The Origin of the Giants

{From such a race as these were.
  This accursed race
Multiplies very greatly;
[And] dispersed throughout the land
And made holes in the ground;
They have big walls built around them
And [have them] surrounded by ditches;
They dwelt on hillsides
Where they expected to be safer.
{In many of the places the great walls
{That these [people] built are still visible there,
But many have now tumbled down
Through tempest and storm.
These people held the land
Until the Britons came.
This was before God was born,
As I have worked out by calculation
One thousand one hundred and thirty-six years [ago],
You can always be certain of this.
  From the time that the ladies came
When first they took the land,
Until the time that Brutus came
And took away the name [of] Albion,
And then called it Britain,
Just as the chronicle relates
Adds up to two hundred and sixty [years];
For all this time, this leads [one] to believe,
The giants held the land.

Mes quant cele gent desraee
En terre fust multipliee,
Chescun divers pays prist
Ou sa manauntie fist ;
E la vesquy chescun par sei
En tiel orgoil e tiel desrai   500
Qe chescun a sun poer
Voleit autre sourmounter.
Car chescun tant se affioit
En la force q'il avoit
Qe nul de eux autre ne dota,
Mes chescun autre despisa,
E chescun vencre bien quida,
E tost a ceo s'aparailla,
Pur conquere par mestrie
La terre e la seignurie.   510
Tantost entre eux sourdi contek,
Chescun a autre fist eschek,
Sovent se entremedlerent.
E sovent se entretuerent.
Tant sovent se cumbatoient
Qe de touz ne remanoient
Fors soulement vint e quatre
Qe vindrent a Brut cumbatre
Quant primes la terre prist.
Mes Brut trestouz les desconfit,   520
Sauf un, qe fust lur avowee,
Qi Gogmagog fu nomee,

THE ORIGIN OF THE GIANTS

But when this race quarrelled[79]
They were multiplied around the land,
Each one took a different [part of the] land
Where he settled;
And lived there each one for himself
With such pride and such violence
{That each one wanted
{To subject another to his authority.
For each one had so much faith
In the strength that he had
That none of them feared another,
But each one despised the other[s],
And each one really thought that he could win
And soon prepared himself for this
To conquer by force
The land and lordship of it.
Soon discord arose among them,
Each one pillaged another
Sometimes they joined battle
And sometimes they killed each other.
They fought each other so often
{That of all of them
{ Only four and twenty remain
Who fight against Brutus
When he first took the land.
But Brutus defeated them all,
Apart from one, who was their leader,
Who was called Gogmagog,

---

[79] Lit: 'Became unruly'

A qi la vie Brut dona ;
Car mult de li s'enmerveilla
E de la grandour q'il avoit
– Car de .xx. peez de long estoit –
E de li voleit enquere
Coment vindrent en la terre,
E dunt, e de quele lignage
Pristrent primes parentage. 530
E il trestut a Brut conta
De lur origne coment ala ;
Coment en la terre vindrent,
E coment aprés se contindrent ;
E cumbien de tens fu passé
Q'en la terre pristrent see ;
E coment furent engendré
De chief en chief li ad counté,
Si cum il einz avoit oy
De ceux qe furent avant li. 540
E Brut trestut fist remembrer,
Qe autres aprés pussent saver
La merveille de la geste
Pur counter a haute feste,
E qe hom puet aver en memoire
La merveille del estoire.
 Oy avez la verité
Come la geste nous ad counté
Quant e coment e dunt cil vindrent
Qi Engleterre primes tindrent, 550

The Origin of the Giants

Whose life Brutus spared;
For there was much in him to marvel about
Both with regard to his size
– For he was twenty feet tall –
And [Brutus] wanted to enquire of him
How they came to the land,
And from whom, and from what lineage
They were originally descended.
And he recounted everything to Brutus
How their origin came about;
How they came [to be] in the land,
And how they conducted themselves afterwards;
And how much time had elapsed
[During] which they took up their abode;
And how they had been fathered
From beginning to end he has recounted to him,
Just as he had heard earlier
From those who had [gone] before him.
And Brutus had everything recorded
So that others afterwards would be able to know
The wonders of the chronicle,
In order to [be able to] to tell [of them] at high feast[s],
And that one may know[80]
The wonder of the story.

    You have heard the truth
As the chronicle has narrated to us,
When and how and whence those people came
Who first ruled England,

---

[80] Lit: 'have in the memory'.

E de quel noun estoit nomé
E de par qi li ert doné,
E combien la terre tindrent
Avant ceo qe Bretons vindrent,
E le premer noun osterent,
E Bretaigne la nomerent.
Tut est bon a remembrer,
Rien ne grevera de saver
Les diz e les escriptures
Des auncienes aventures. 560
De Dampne-Dieu seit il benet
Qi en escripture les metteit.
      Amen

The Origin of the Giants

And after whose name it was called,
And by whom it was given,
And how long they ruled the land
Before the Britons came,
And removed the first name,
And named it Britain.
It is good to record everything, [81]
It will do no harm to know
The utterances and writings
About what happened in ancient times.
{May he who put these these [things] down in writing
{Be blessed by the Lord God.
    Amen

---

[81] Lit: 'All is good to record'

Bibliography and further reading

Editions of Dez Grantz Geanz

Brereton, Georgine E. *Dez Grantz Geanz: An Anglo-Norman Poem*. Medium Ævum Monographs II. Oxford: Basil Blackwell, 1937.

Carley, James P. and Crick, Julia. 'Constructing Albion's Past: an Annotated Edition of De Origine Gigantum'. *Arthurian Literature* XIII (1995): 41–114.

Jubinal, Achille. 'Des graunz jaianz qui primes conquistrent Bretaigne.' *Nouveau recueil des contes, dits, fabliaux, et autres pièces inédites*. 2 vols. Paris: Chez Challamel, 1842: 354-71.

Michel, François. 'De Primis Inhabitatoribus Angliæ'. *Gesta Regum Britanniae*. London: Cambrian Archaeological Association, 1862: 199–214.

Primary Sources

Barron, W.R.J and Burgess Glyn S. *The Voyage of Saint Brendan: Representative Versions of the Legend in English Translation*. Exeter: University of Exeter Press, 2005.

Heaney, Seamus (trans.). *Beowulf: Bilingual Edition*. London: Faber and Faber, 2007.

Geoffrey of Monmouth. *The History of the Kings of Britain*. Ed. Michael D Reeve. Trans. Neil Wright. Woodbridge: The Boydell Press, 2007.

Gildas, *The Ruin of Britain and Other Documents*. Ed. and Trans. Michael Winterbottom. Arthurian Sources Vol. 7. London: Phillimore and Co: 1978.

Marsden, Richard ed. *The Cambridge Old English Reader*. Cambridge: Cambridge University Press, 2004.

Nennius. *British History and the Welsh Annals*. Ed and trans. John Morris. Arthurian Sources Vol. 8. London: Phillimore and Co: 1980.

The Origin of the Giants

Virgil, *The Aeneid*. Trans. Frederick Ahl. Oxford: Oxford University Press, 2007.

Weiss, Judith (ed. and trans). *Wace's Roman de Brut: A History of the British*. Revised ed. Exeter: University of Exeter Press, 2002.

Secondary Sources

Aurell, Martin. 'Geoffrey of Monmouth's History of the Kings of Britain and the Twelfth-Century Renaissance'. Ed. Stephen Morillo. *The Haskins Society Journal*. Vol. 18. Woodbridge, the Boydell Press, 2006: 1–18.

Bates, Sarah. *The New History of the Trojan Wars and Troy's Destruction in Four Books*. London: Printed for Sarah Bates at the Sun and Bible in Giltspur Street; and James Hodges at the Looking Glass on London Bridge, 1735.

Bernau, Anke. 'Beginning with Albina: Remembering the Nation'. *Exemplaria* 21 (2009): 247–73.

Boreman, Thomas. *The Gigantick History of the Two Famous Giants, and other Curiosities in Guildhall, London*. 3rd ed. London: Printed for Thomas Boreman, 1741.

Brown, Theo. 'The Trojans in Devon'. *Report and Transactions of the Devonshire Association for the Advancement of Science, Literature and Art* (1955): 63–76.

Byrne, Mary E 'On the Punishment of Sending Adrift'. *Ériu* 11 (1932): 97–102.

Cohen, Jeffrey Jerome. *Of Giants: Sex, Monsters, and the Middle Ages*. London and Minneapolis: University of Minnesota Press.

Drukker, Tamar. 'Thirty-Three Murderous Sisters: A Pre-Trojan Foundation Myth in the Middle English Brut Chronicle'. *The Review of English Studies*. New Series, Vol. 54 (2003): 449–63.

Frankis, P.J. 'The Thematic Significance of enta geweorc and related imagery in The Wanderer'. *Anglo-Saxon England* 2 (1973): 253–69.

Fuller, Thomas. *The Church History of Britain; From the Birth of Jesus Christ until the Year 1648*. London: Printed for Iohn Williams at the Signe of the Crown in St Paul's Church-yard, 1655.

Halsall, Guy. *Worlds of Arthur*. Oxford: Oxford University Press, 2013.

Jankulak, Karen. *Geoffrey of Monmouth*. Cardiff: University of Wales Press, 2010.

Johnson, Lesley. 'Return to Albion'. *Arthurian Literature* XIII (1995): 19–40

Kaske, R.E. 'Beowulf and the Book of Enoch'. *Speculum* 46.3 (1971): 421–31.

Kiessling, Nicolas, *The Incubus in English Literature: Provenance and Progeny. Pullman:* Washington State University Press, 1977.

Lodge, R Anthony. *French: From Dialect to Standard*. London: Routledge, 1993.

Mackley, J.S. 'English Foundation Myths as Political Empowerment' *Creating Myths as Narratives of Empowerment and Disempowerment*. Jendouba: University of Jendouba Press, forthcoming 2015.

Mackley, J.S. 'Gog and Magog: Guardians of the City'. *London Gothic*. Ed. Lawrence Phillips and Anne Witchard. London: Continuum, 2010.

Marvin, Julia. 'Albine and Isabelle: Regicidal Queens and the Historical Imagination of the Anglo-Norman Prose Brut Chronicles' in *Arthurian Literature* XVIII (2001): 143–91.

Orchard, Andy. *Pride and Prodigies*. Toronto: University of Toronto Press, 2003.

Reinhard, J.R. 'Setting Adrift in Medieval Law and Literature'. *PMLA* 56 (1941): 33–68.

Ruch, Lisa M. *Albina and her Sisters: The Foundation of Albion*. New York: Cambria Press, 2013.

Simons, Walter. *Cities of Ladies: Beguine Communities in the Medieval Low Countries, 1200-1565*. Philadelphia: University of Pennsylvania Press, 2003.

Scherb, Victor I. 'Assimilating Giants: The Appropriation of Gog and Magog in Medieval and Early Modern England'. *Journal of Medieval and Early Modern Studies* 32 (2002): 59–84.

Sinistrari, Ludovico Maria. *Demoniality*. Trans. Isidor Lisieux. Paris: Isidor Liseux, 1879.

Strijbosch, Clara, 'The Heathen Giant in the Voyage of St Brendan', *Celtica* 23 (1999): 369–89.

Swan, Laura. *The Wisdom of the Beguines: The Forgotten Story of a Medieval Women's Movement*. New York: BlueBridge, 2014.

Westcote, Thomas. *View of Devonshire in MDCXXX with a Pedigree of Most of its Gentry*. Exeter: William Roberts, 1845.

Westwood, Jennifer and Simpson, Jacqueline. *The Lore of the Land*. London: Penguin Books, 2005.

Withington, Robert. *English Pageantry*. 2 vols. Cambridge: Harvard University Press, 1918.

ABOUT THE AUTHOR

J.S. Mackley is a Senior Lecturer in English and Creative Writing at the University of Northampton. He studied for a degree in English Studies at the University of Stirling, and an MA and PhD in Late Medieval Studies and English, both at the University of York.

He is author of *The Legend of St Brendan: A Comparative Study of the Latin and Anglo-Norman Versions* and *The Anglo-Norman Brendan: Bilingual Edition.* He has recently finished editing a Gothic novel last published in 1802 entitled *Who's the Murderer* by Eleanor Sleath (forthcoming from Valancourt Press). He is also one of the editors of *Creating Myths as Narratives of Empowerment and Disempowerment* (forthcoming from University of Jendouba Press).

He has also written articles on St Brendan, gothic literature, fantasy literature and more recently, English mythology. He is currently working on a translation of a treatise on cosmography.

www.ingramcontent.com/pod-product-compliance
Lightning Source LLC
Chambersburg PA
CBHW071220070526
44584CB00019B/3085